Copyright© 2020 by Saiko Print

All rights reserved. No part of this publication may be reproduced, distributed, or transmitted in any form or by any means, including photocopying, recording, or other electronic methods.

Find us at:
instagram.com/saikoprint
Etsy.com/saikoprint

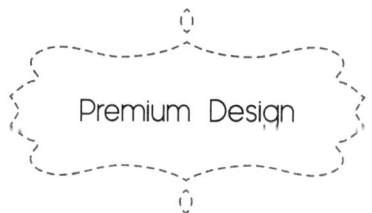

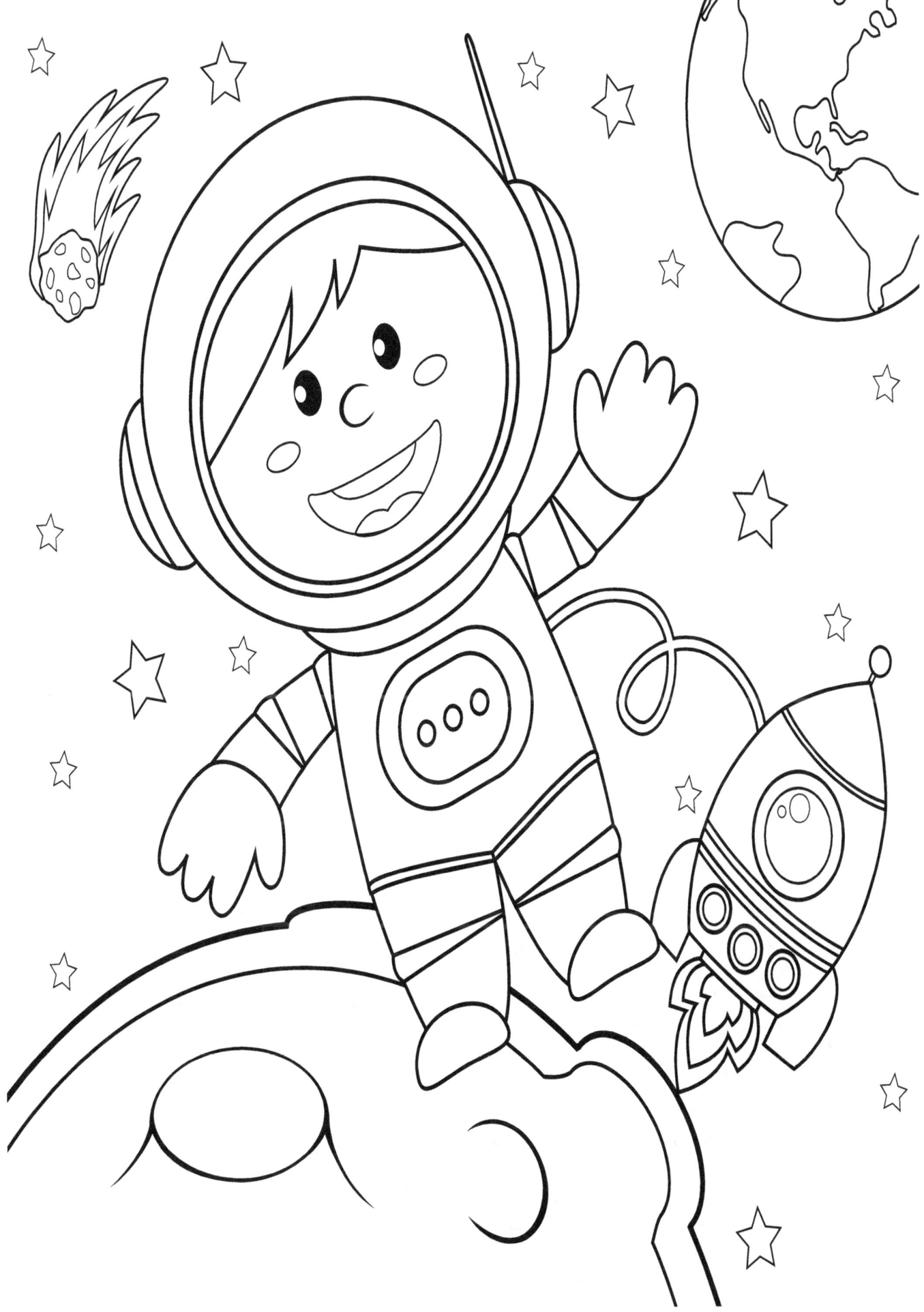

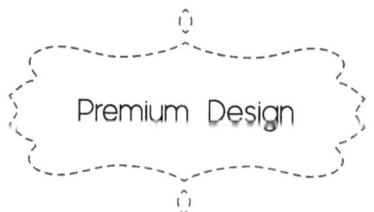

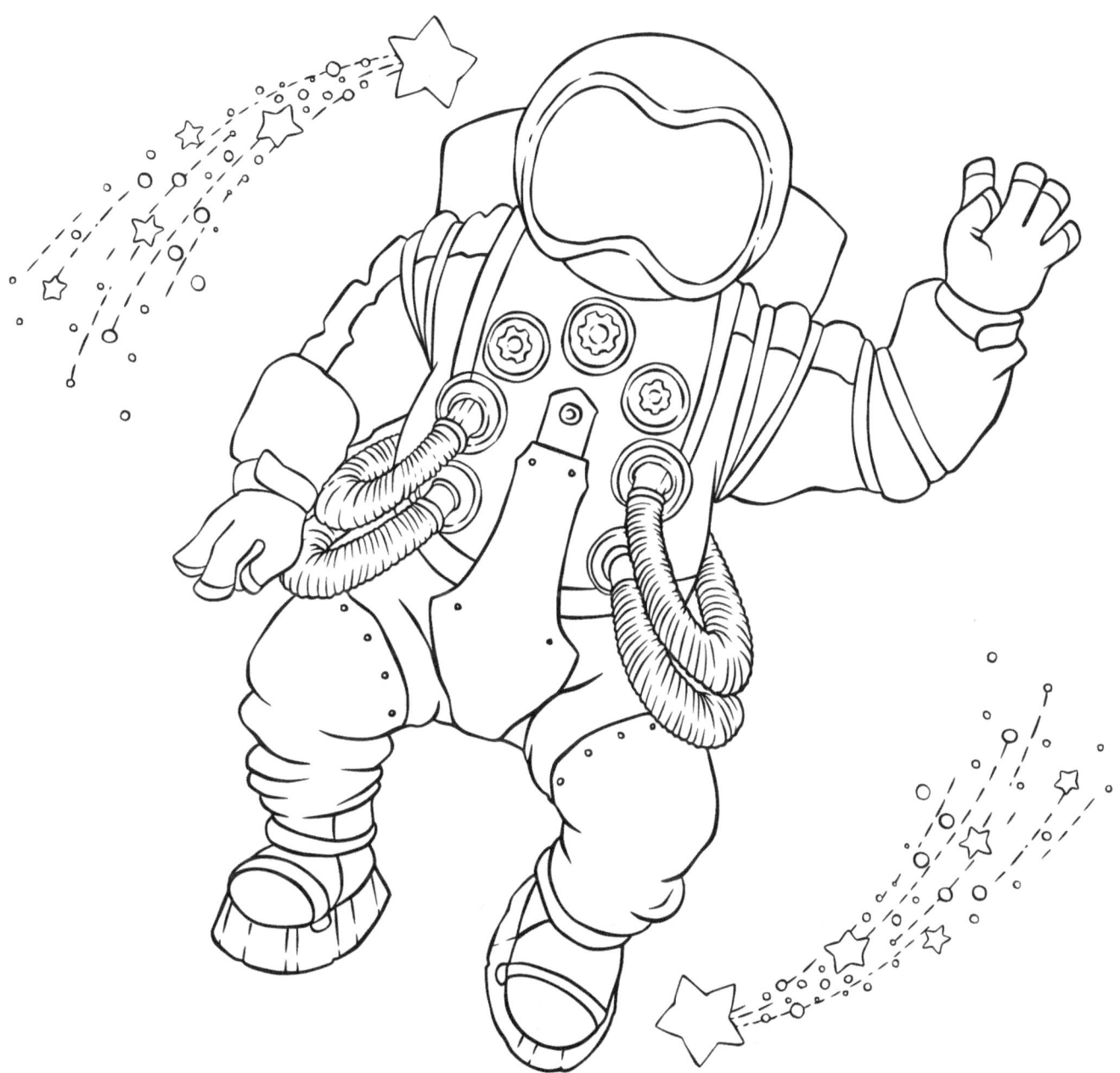

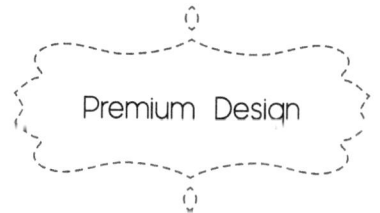

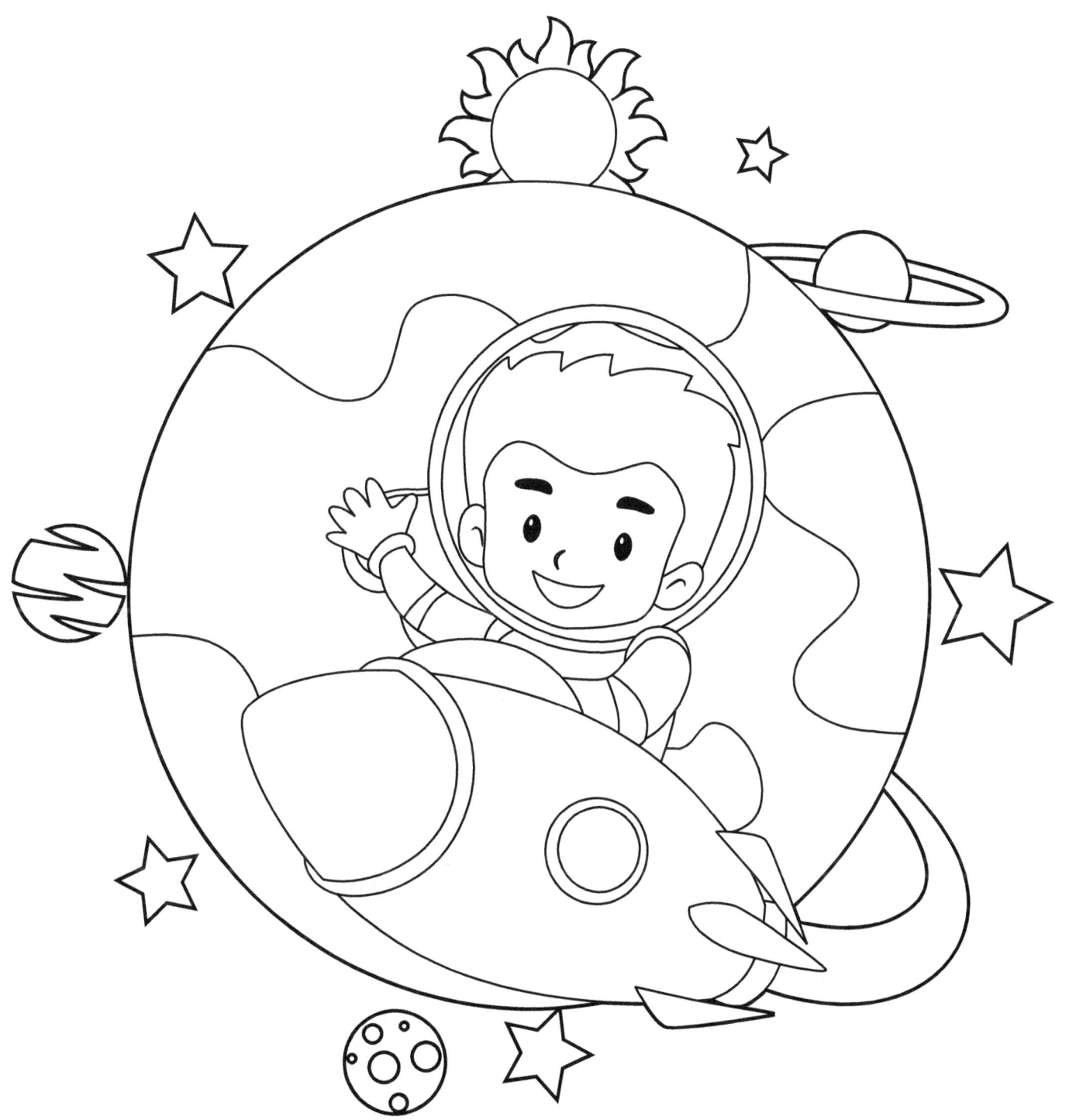

Premium Design

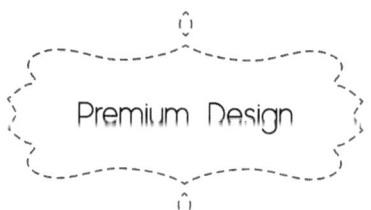

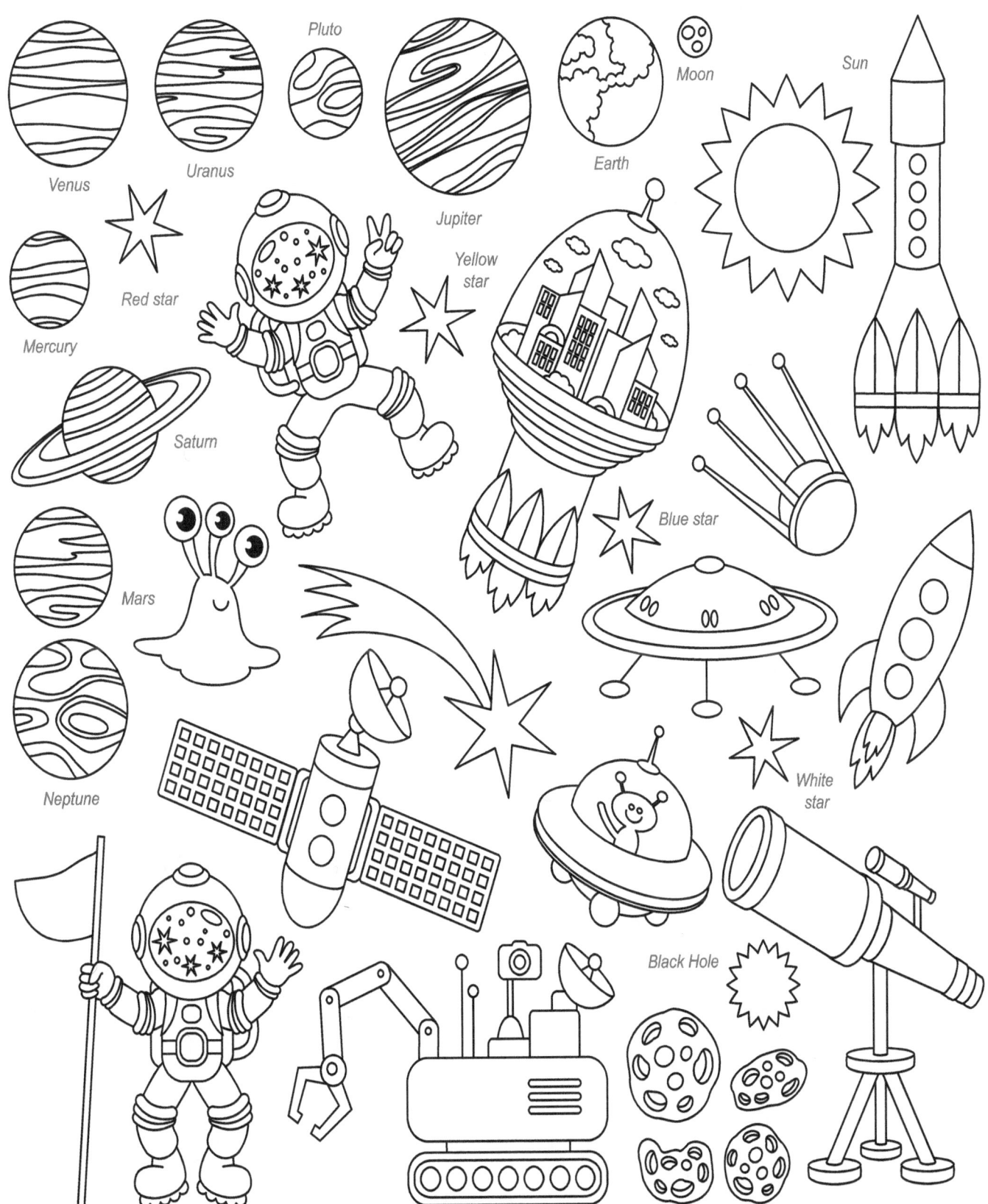

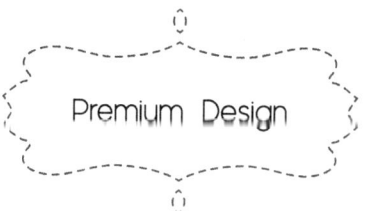

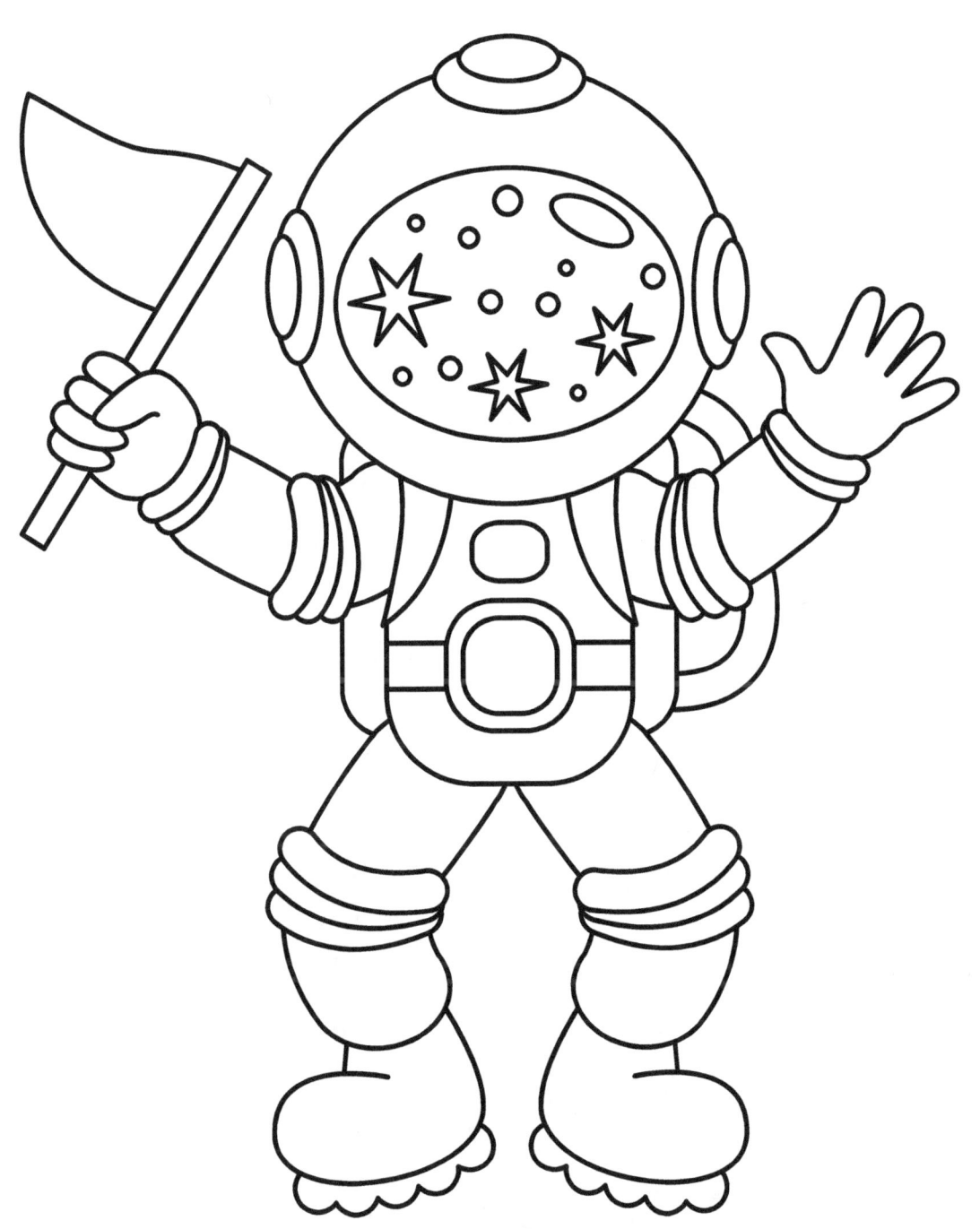

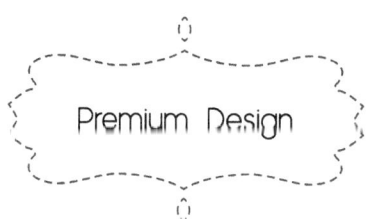

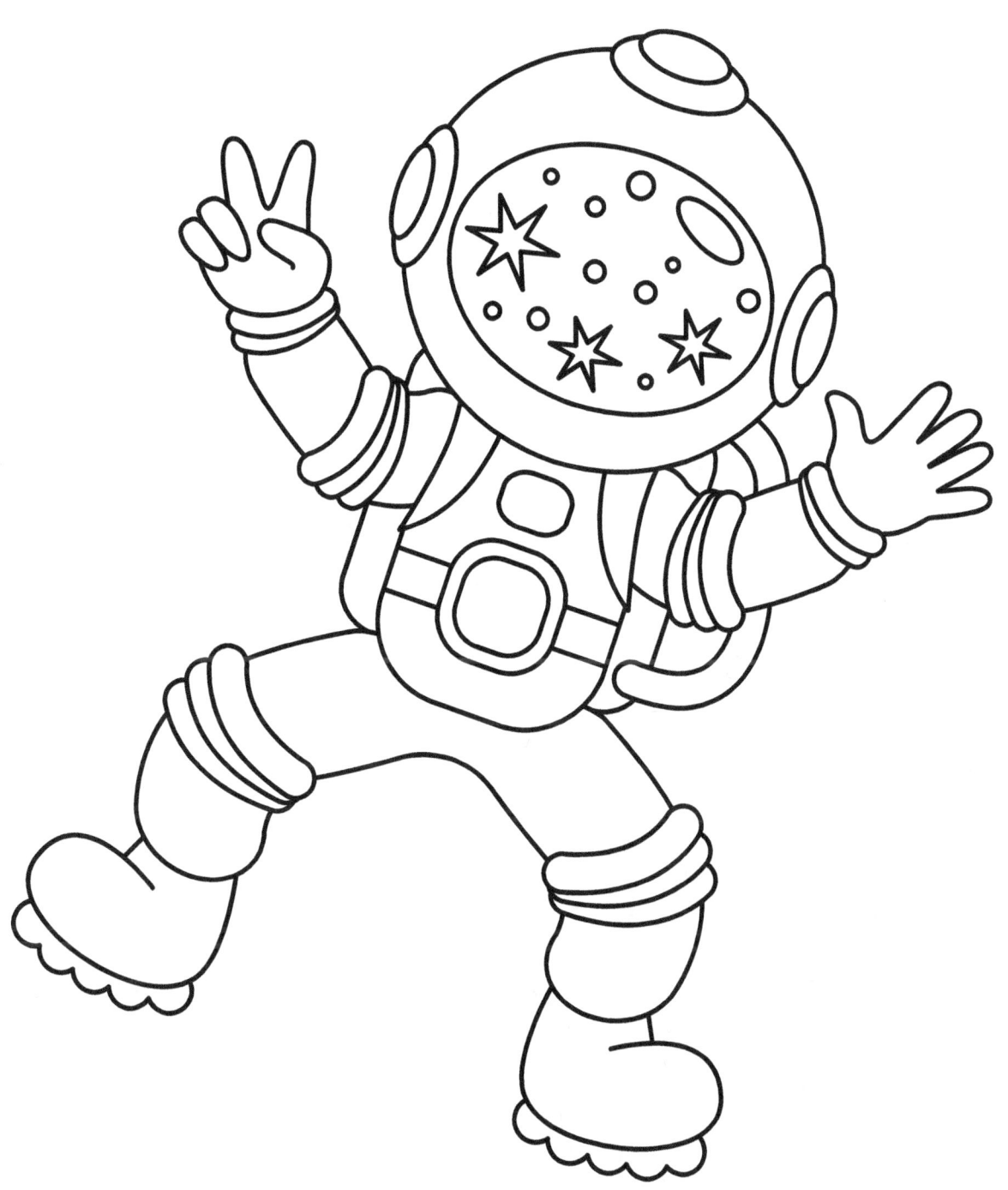

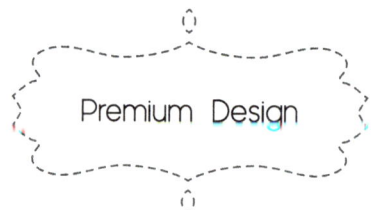

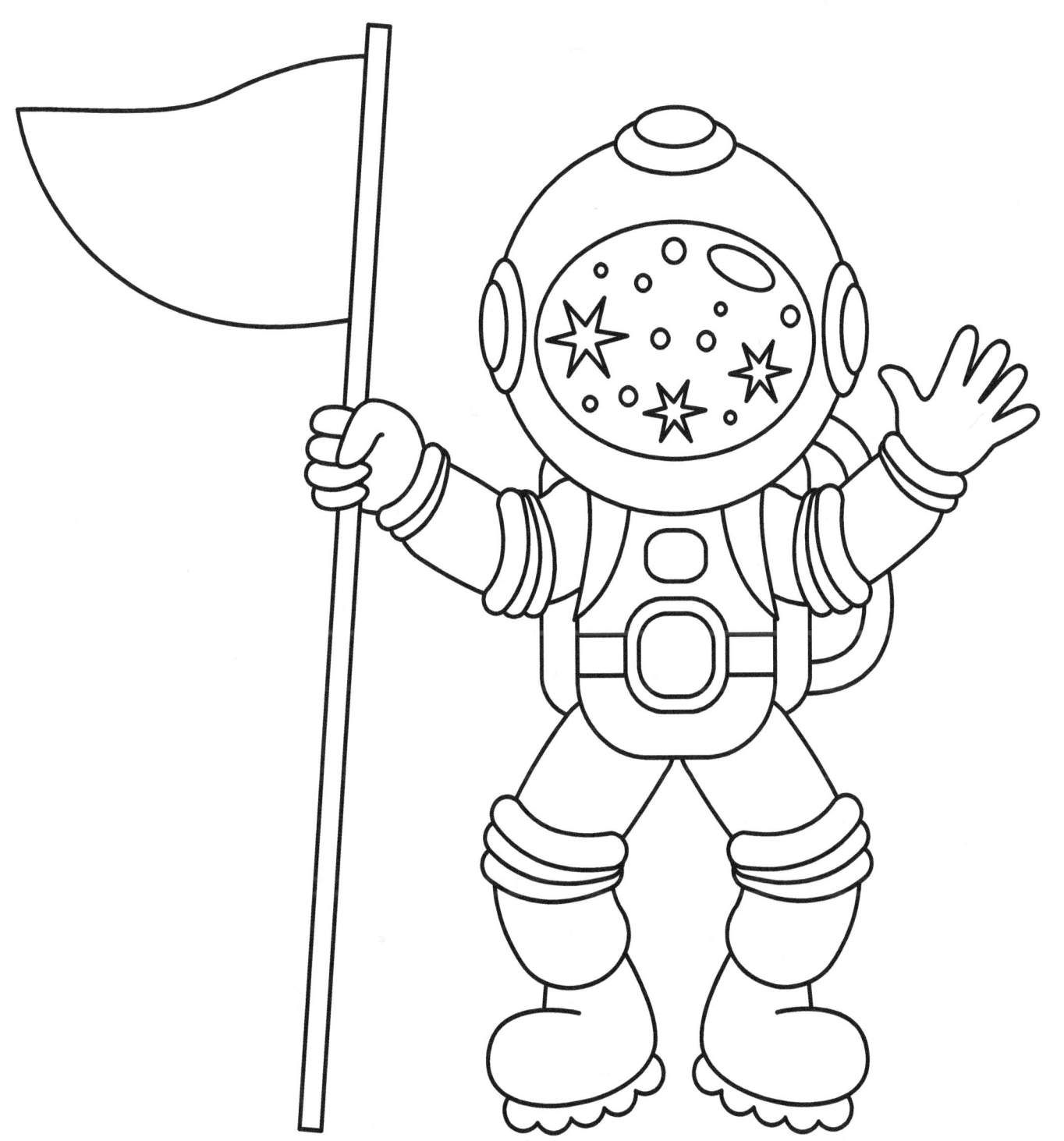

Premium Design

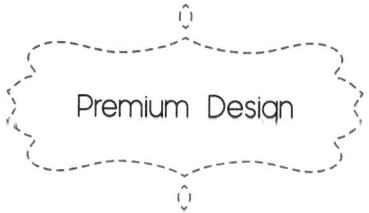

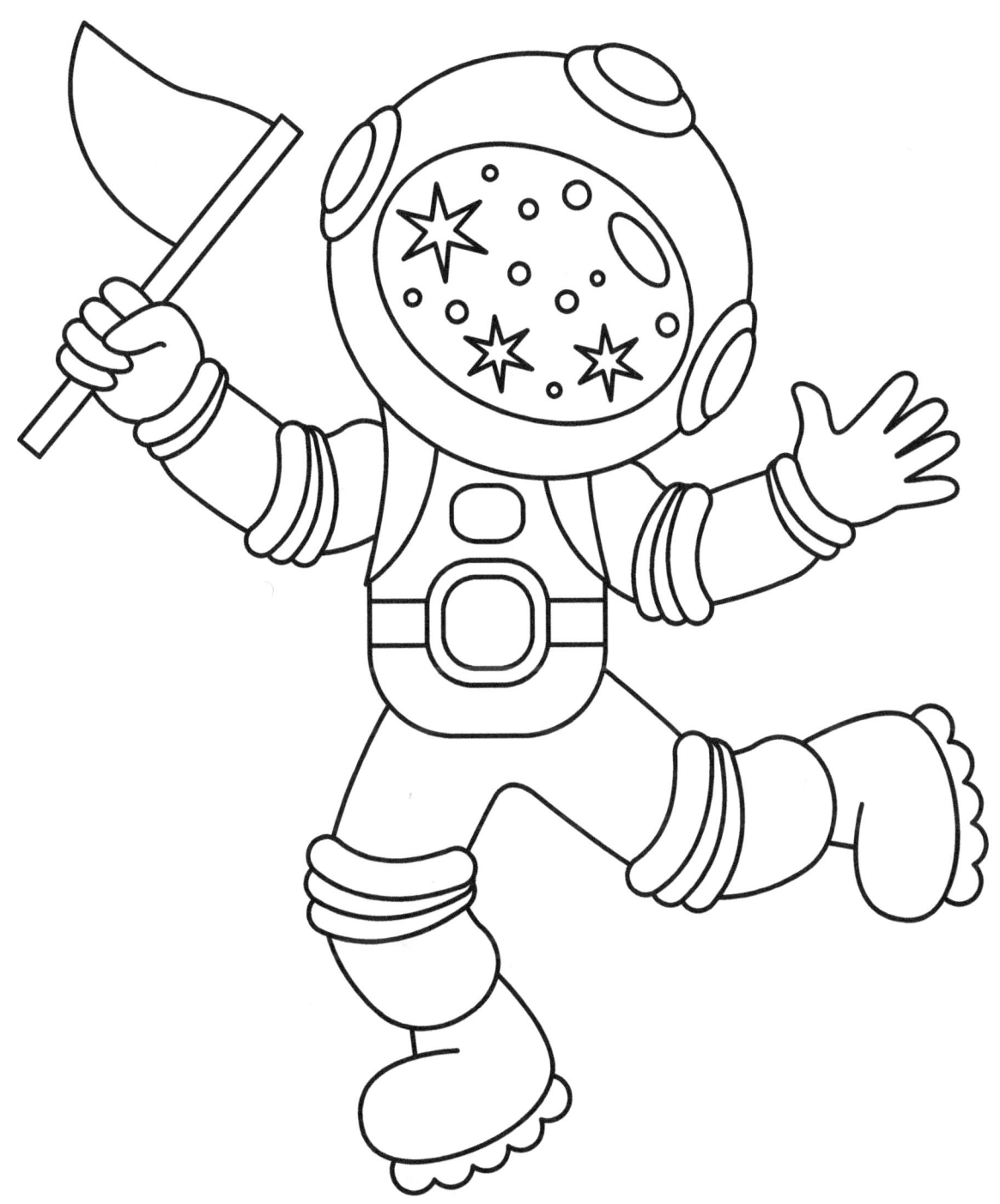

Premium Design

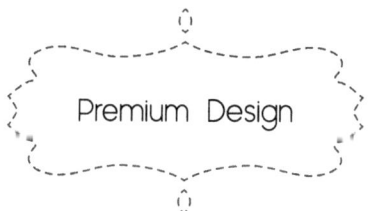

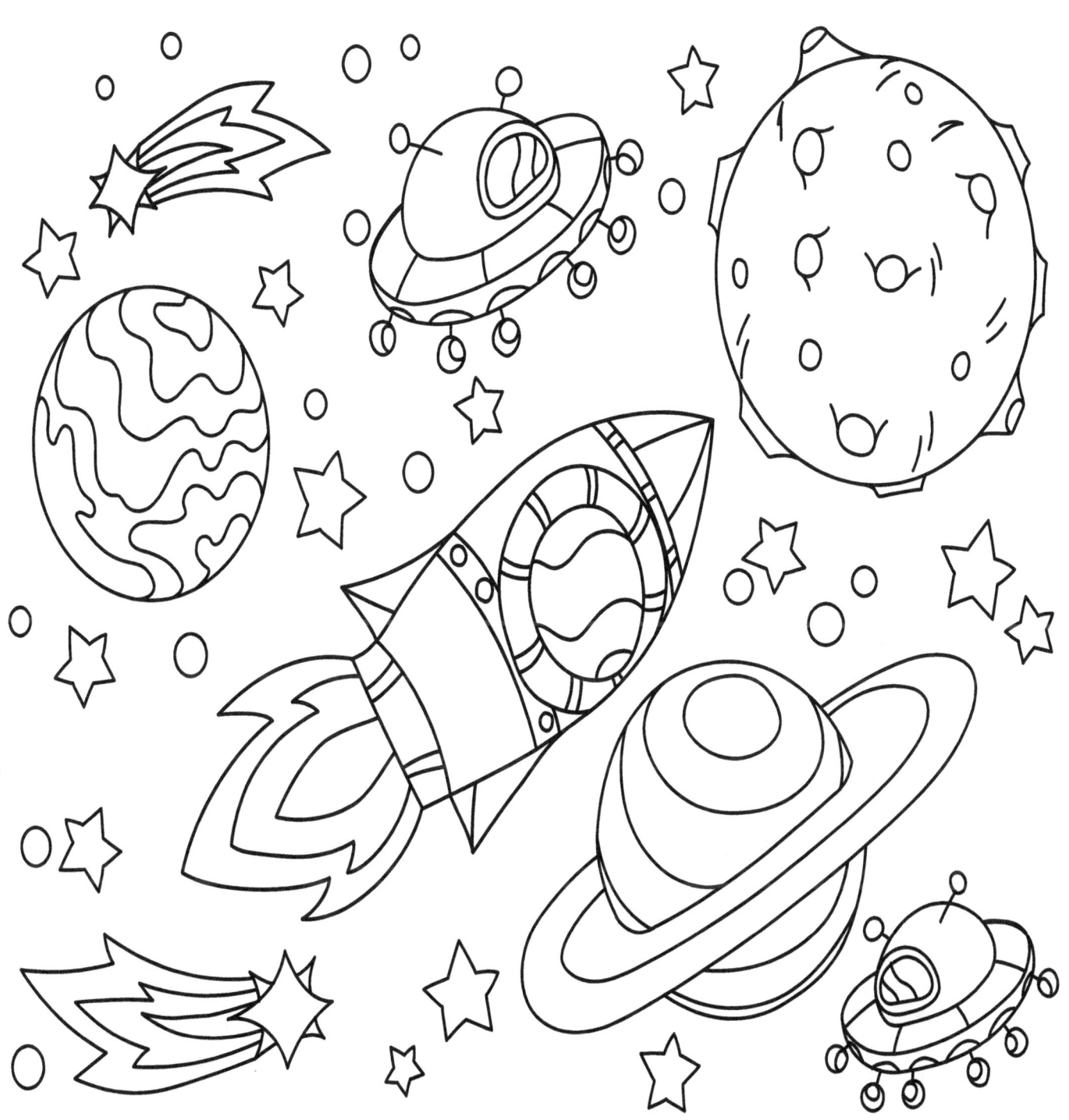

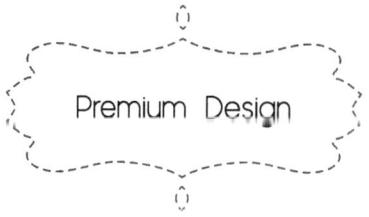

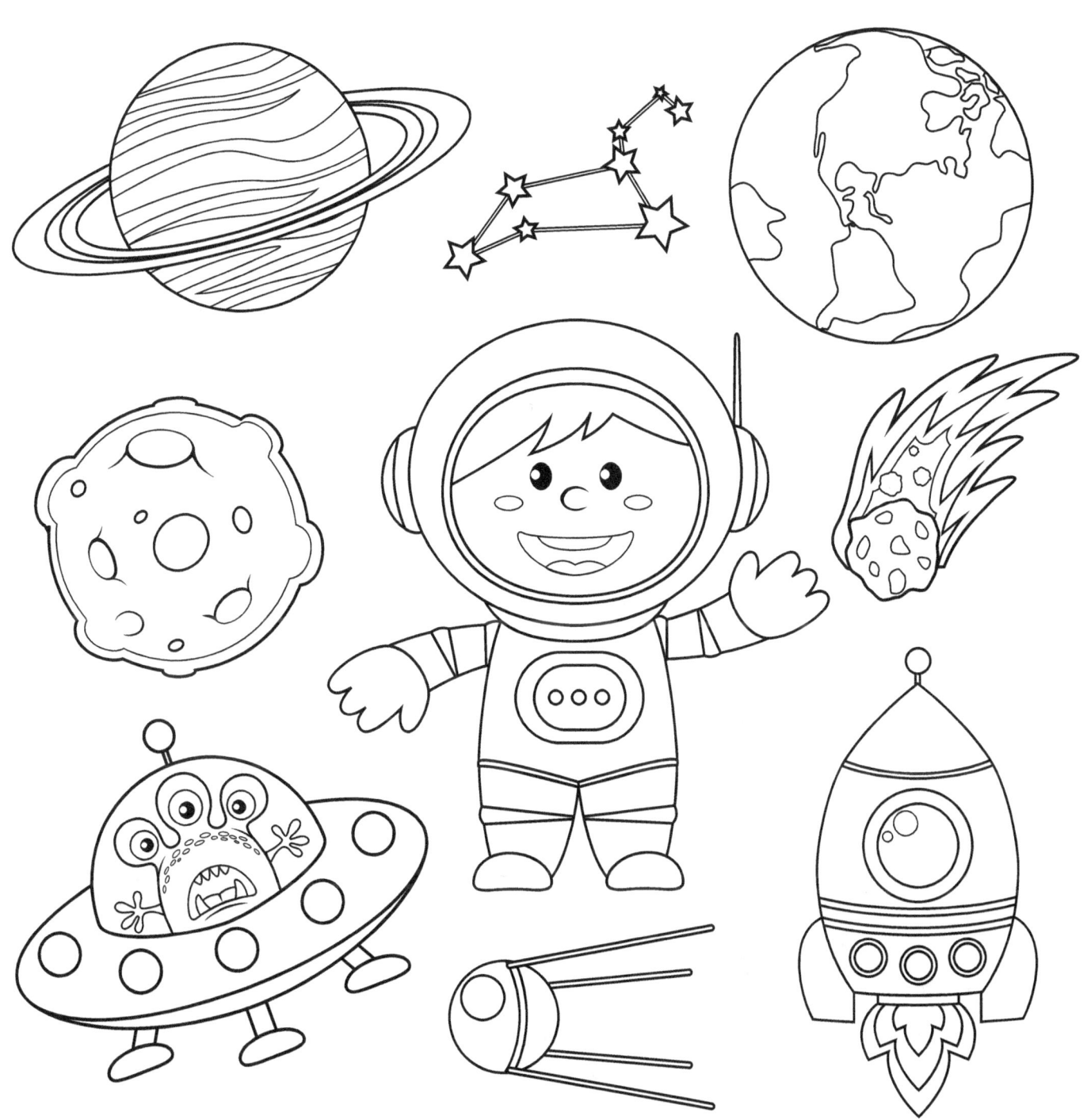

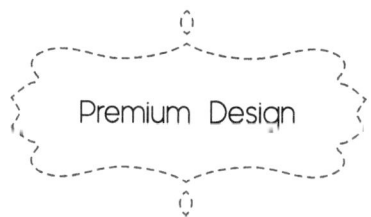

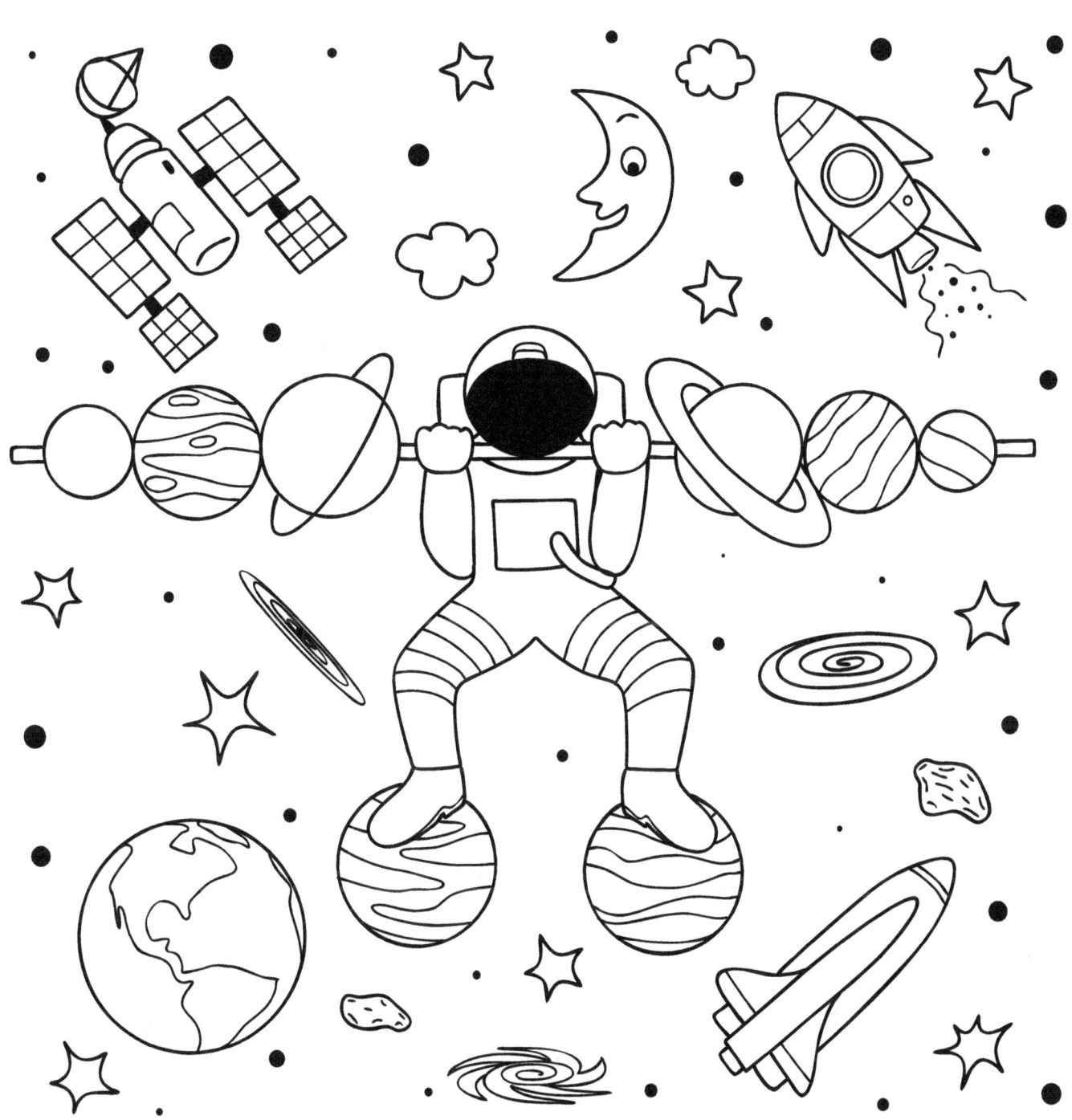

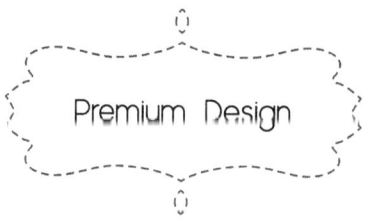

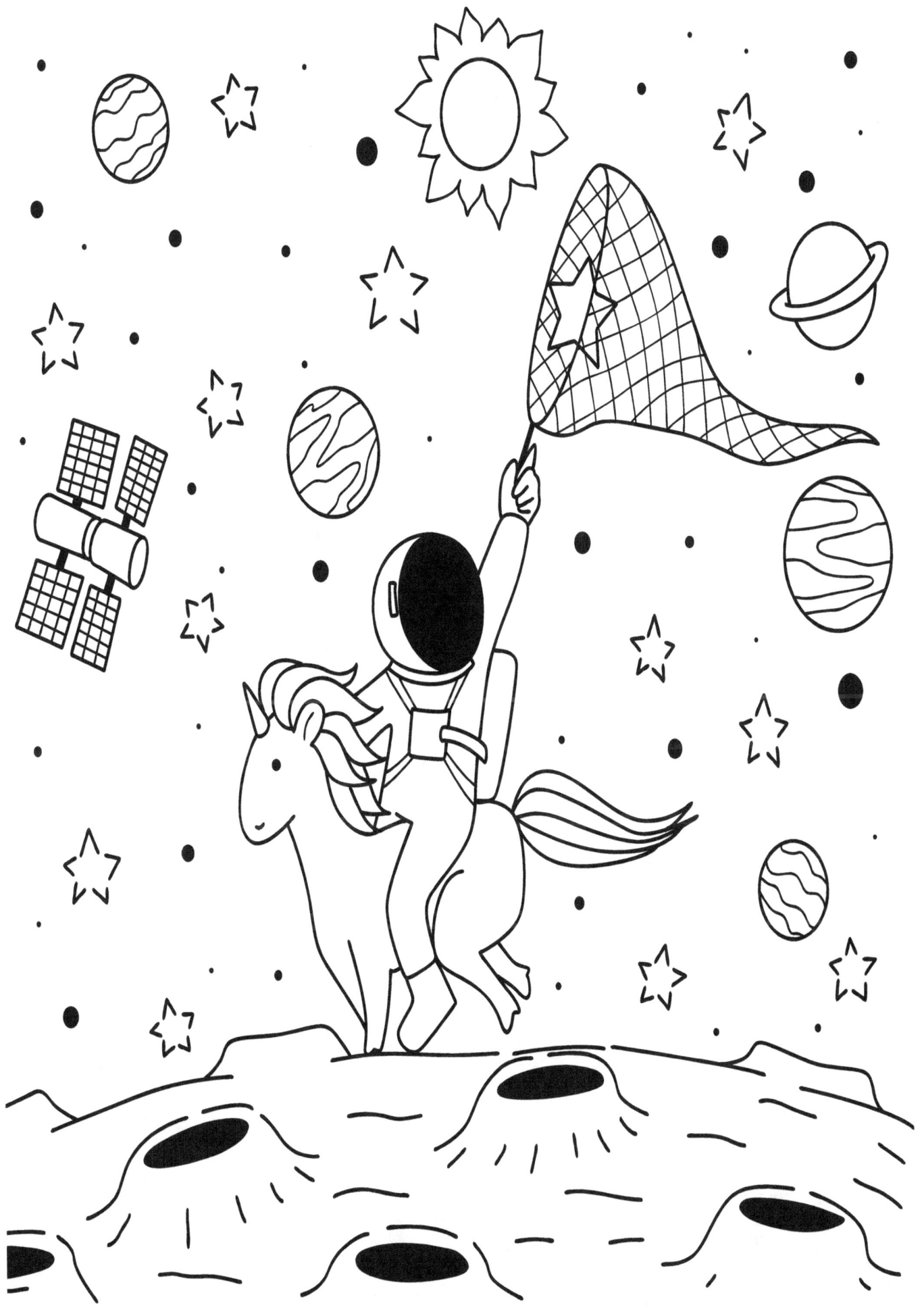

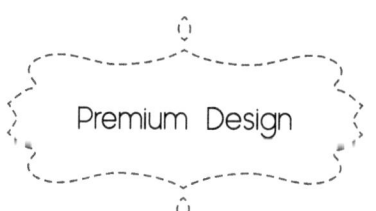

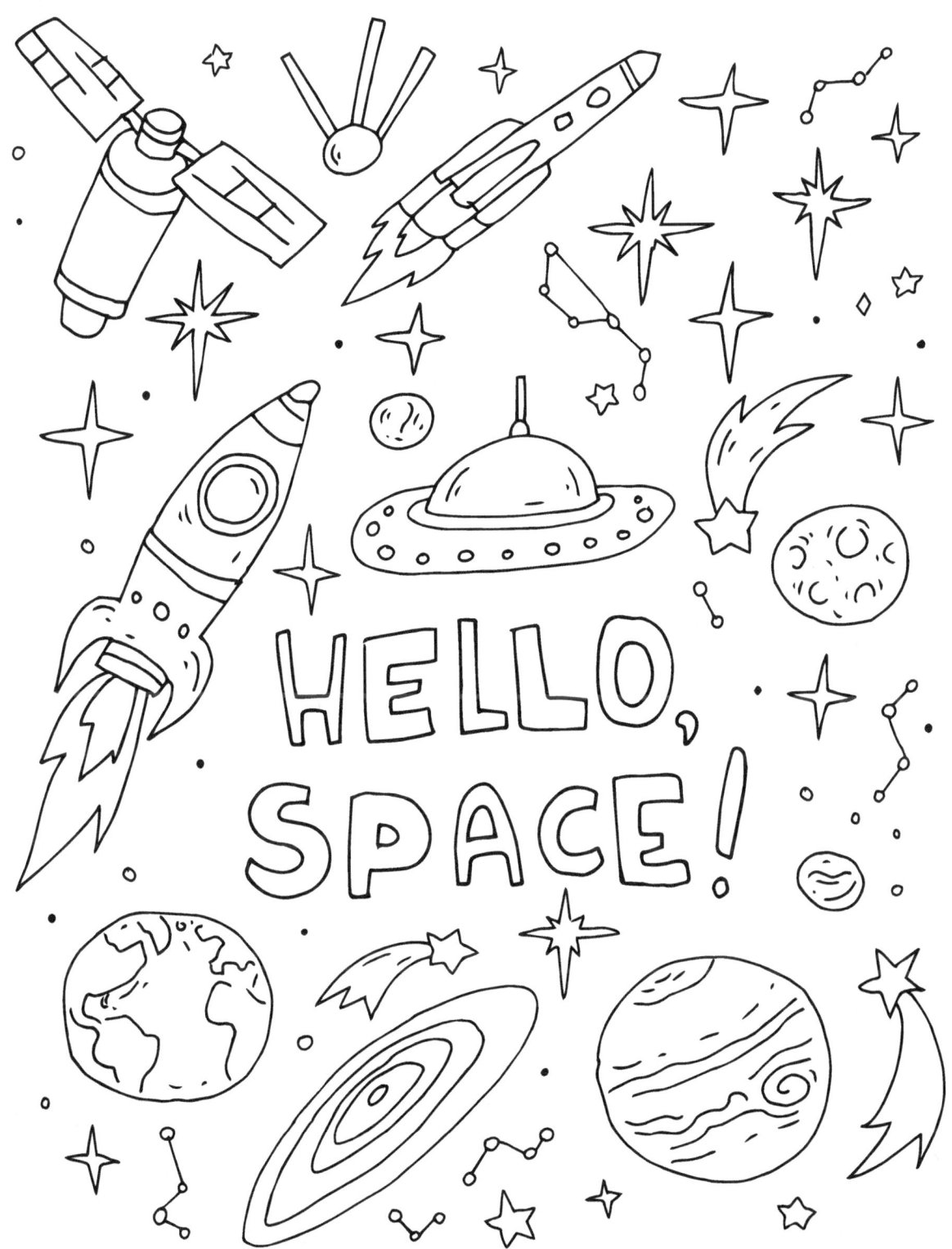

Premium Design

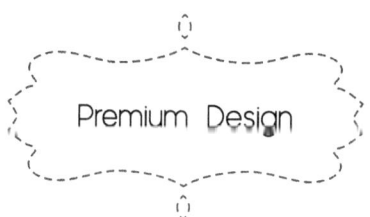

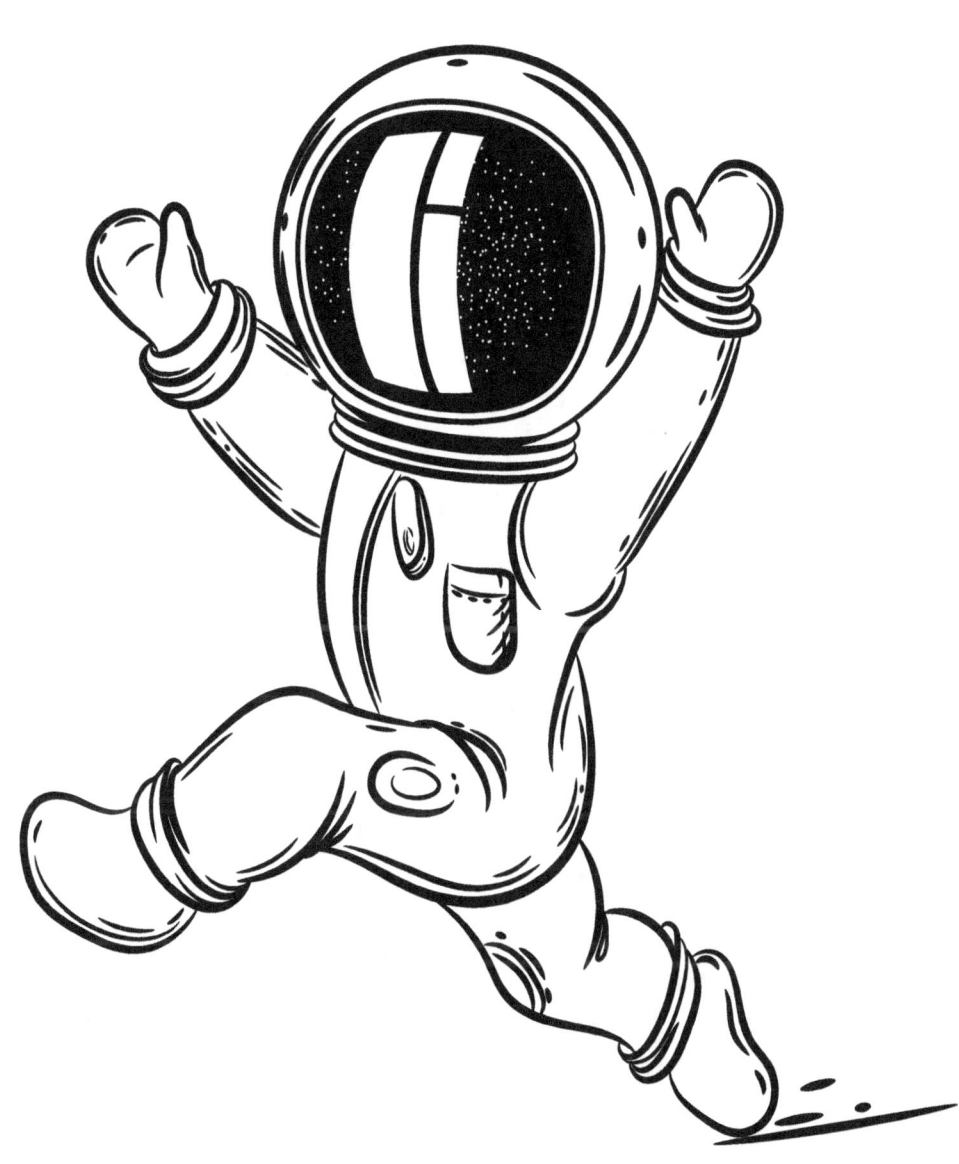

Premium Design

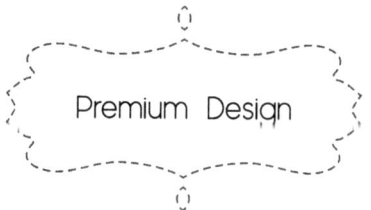

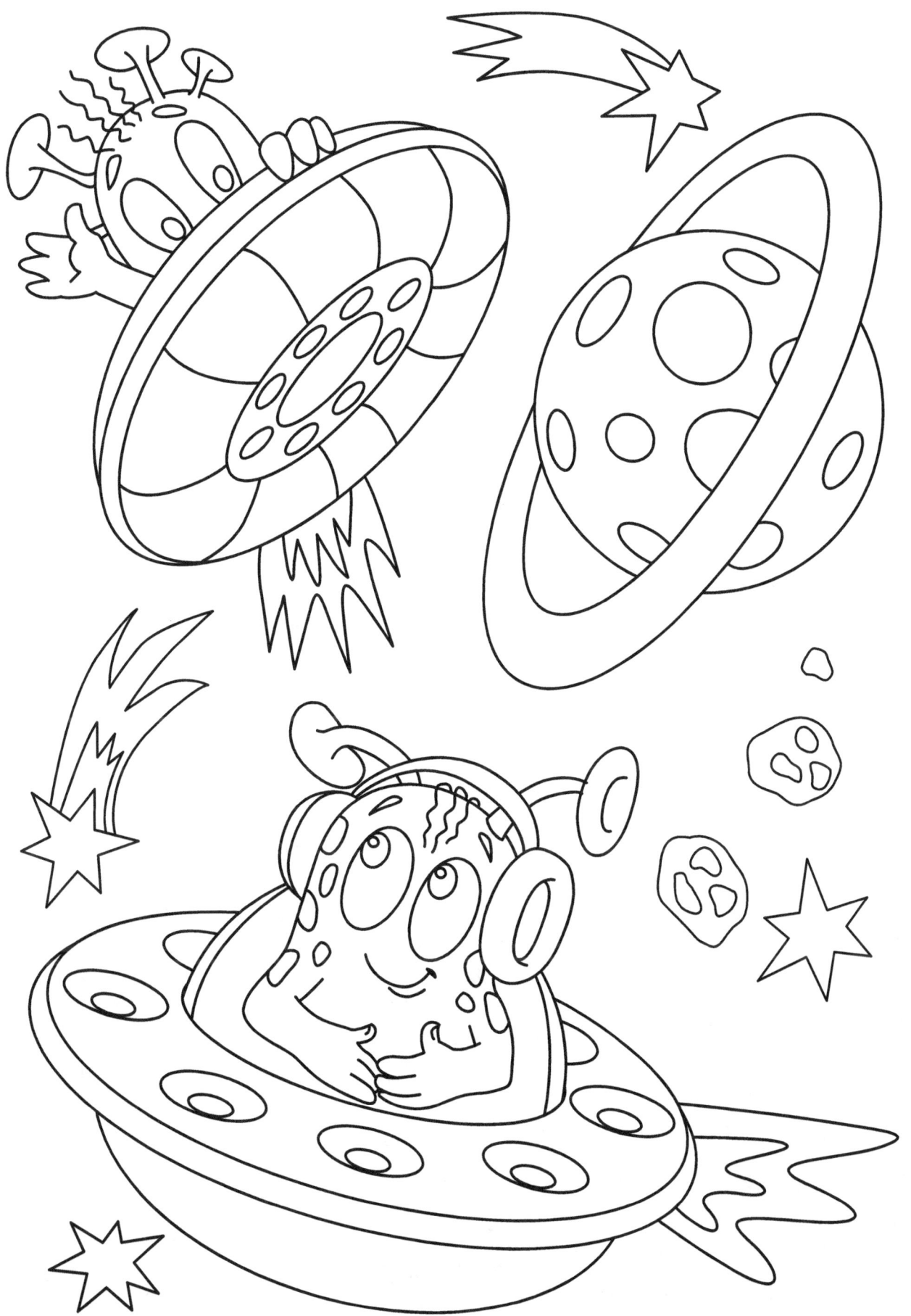

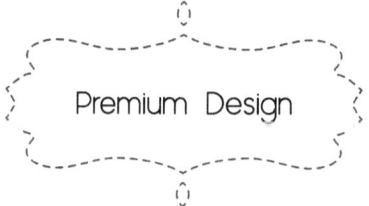

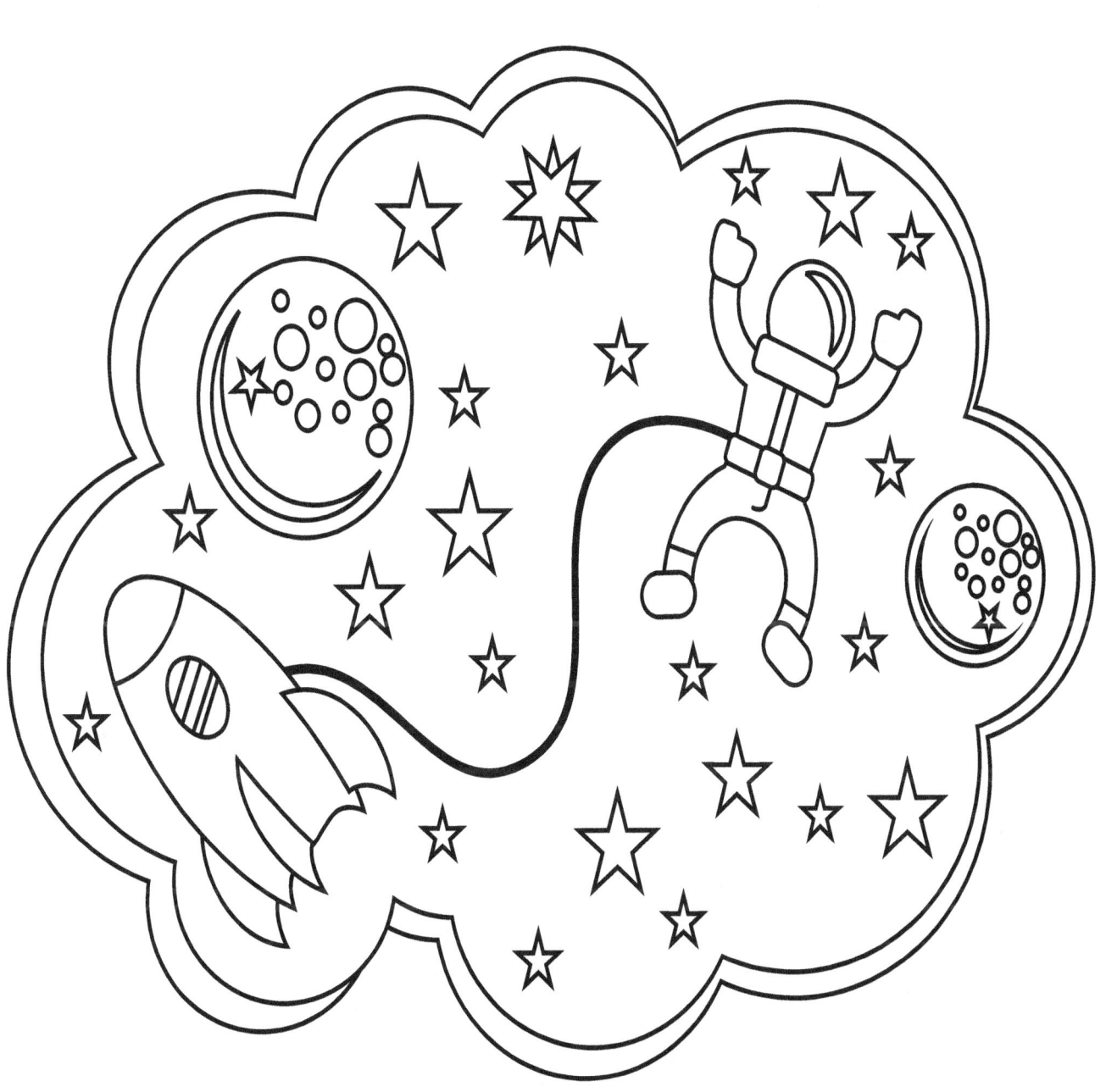

Premium Design

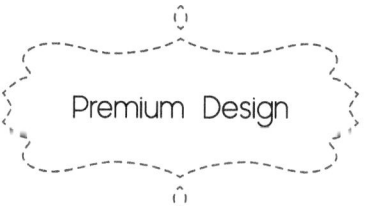

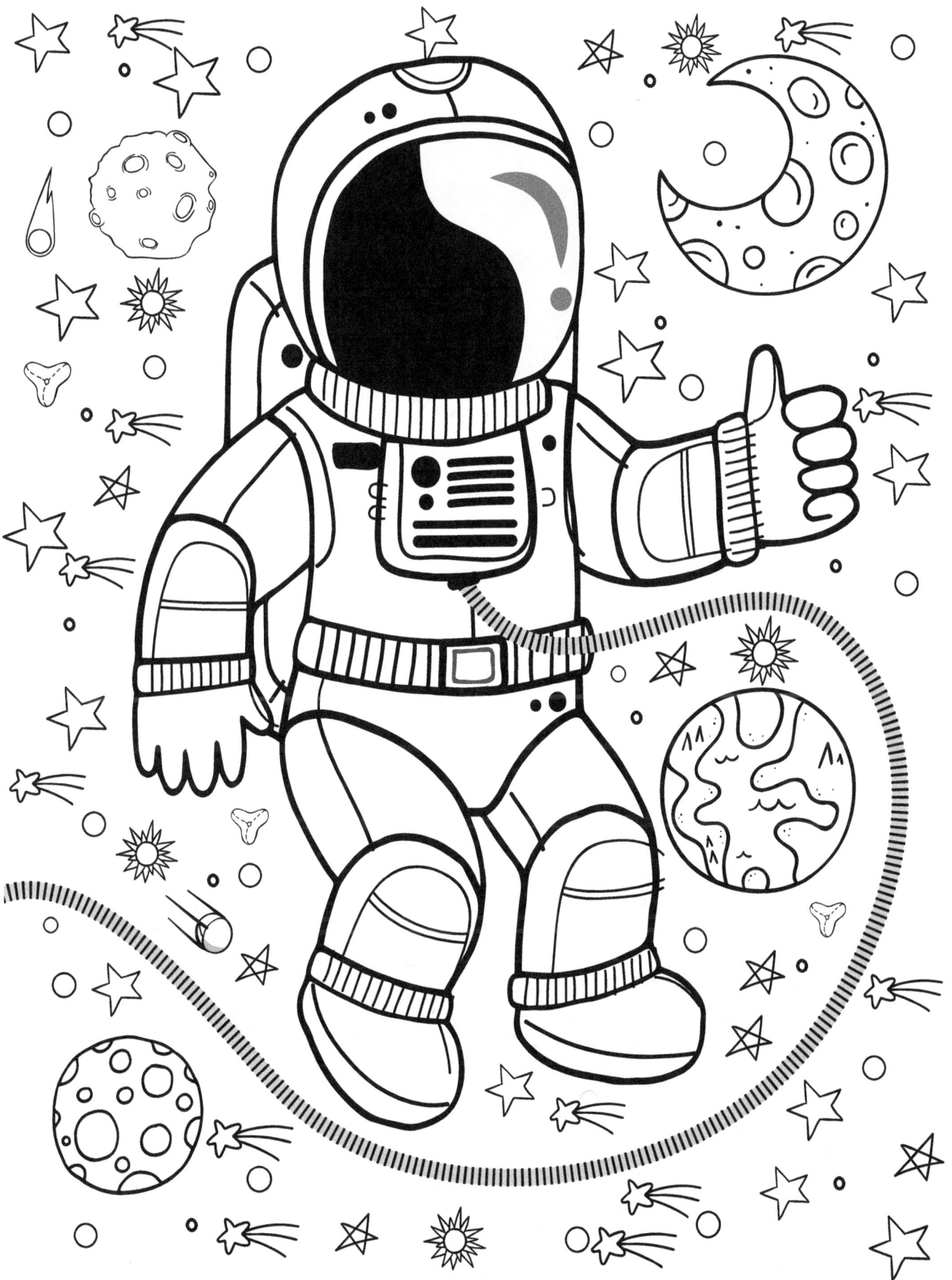

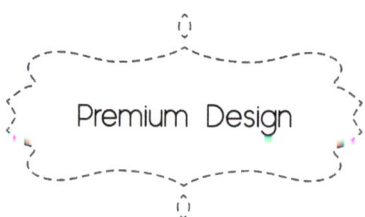

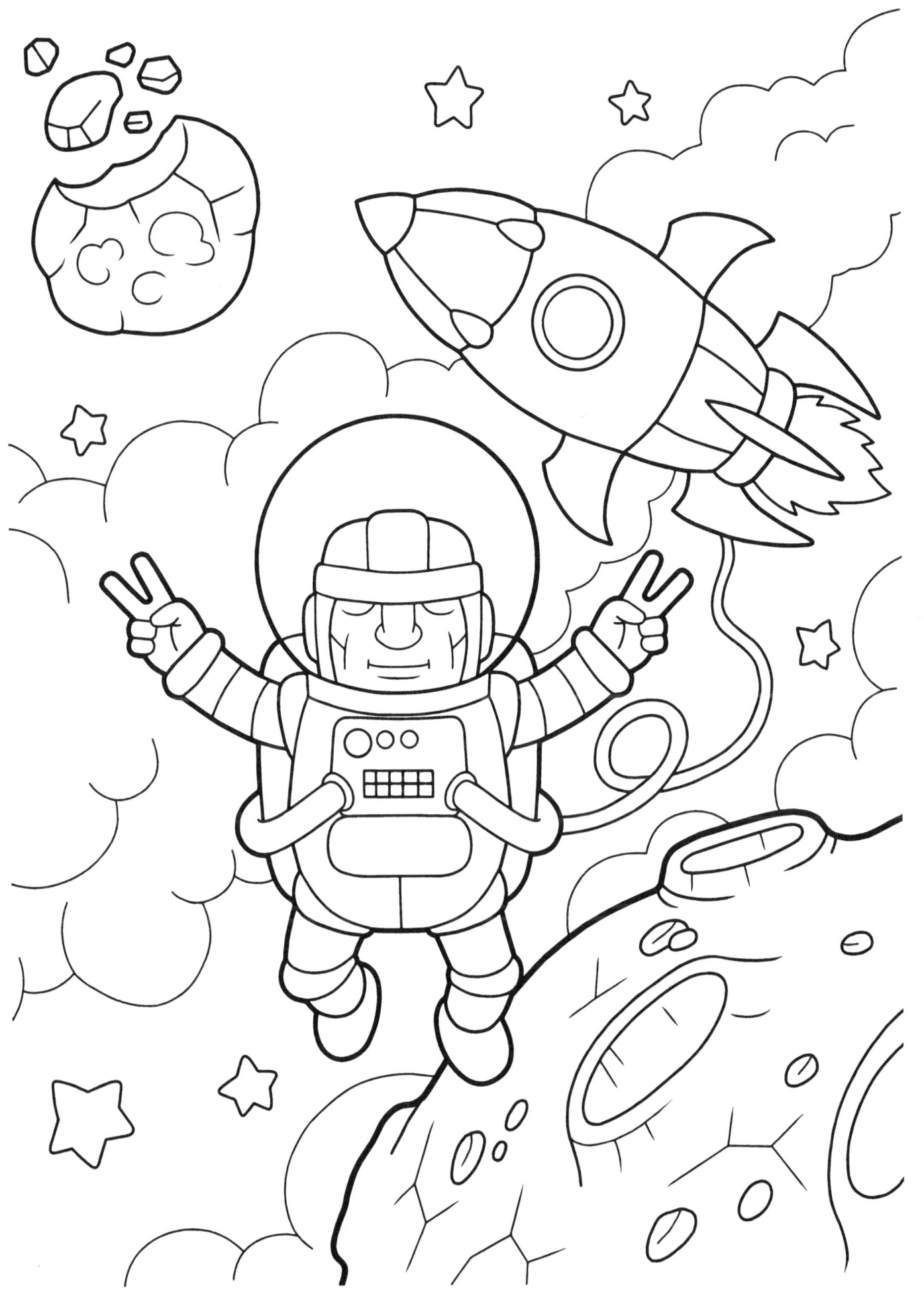

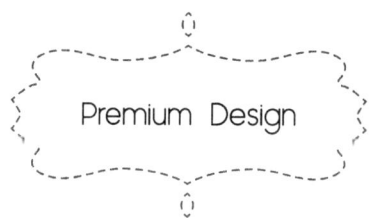

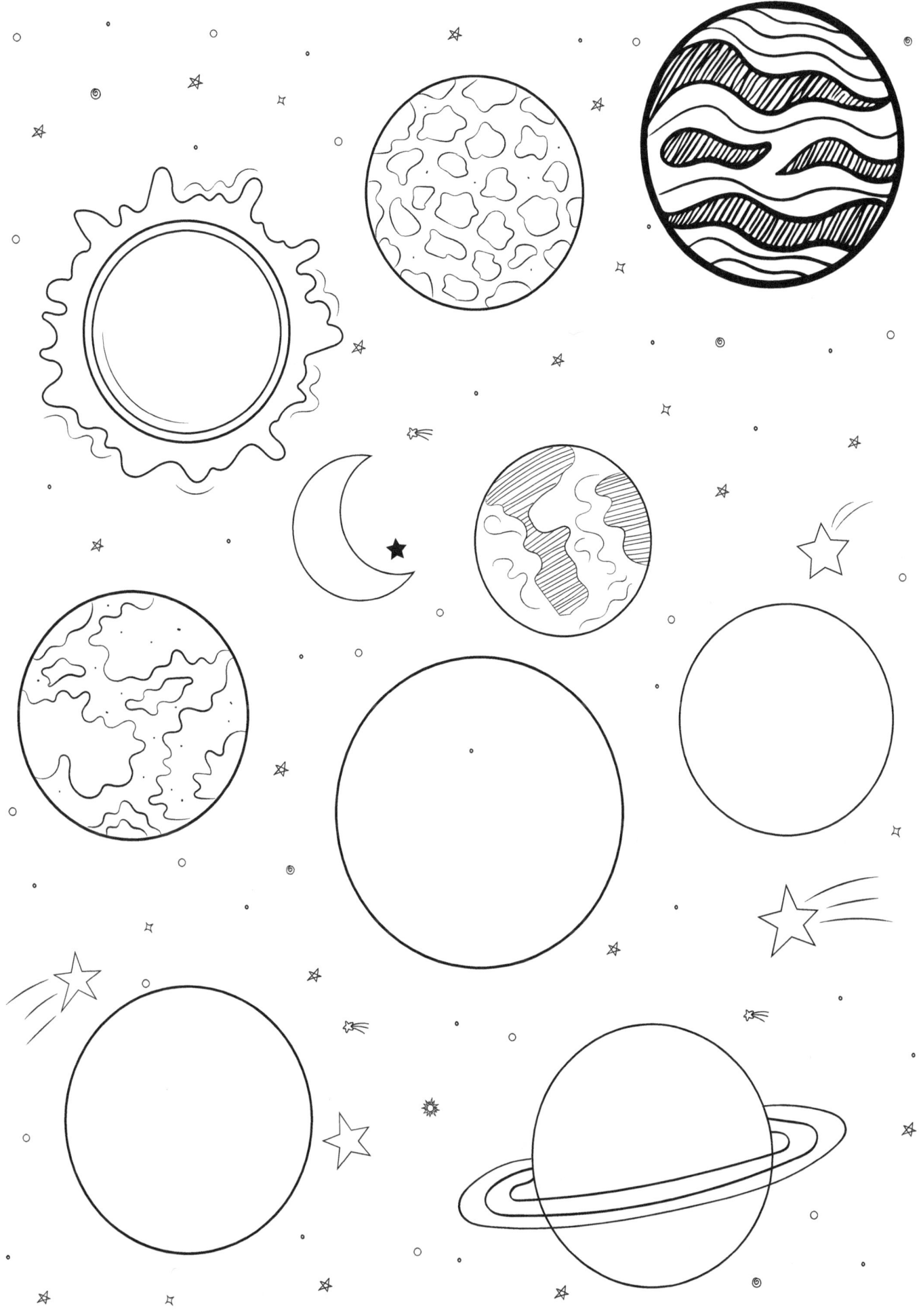

Premium Design

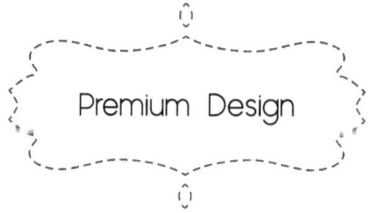

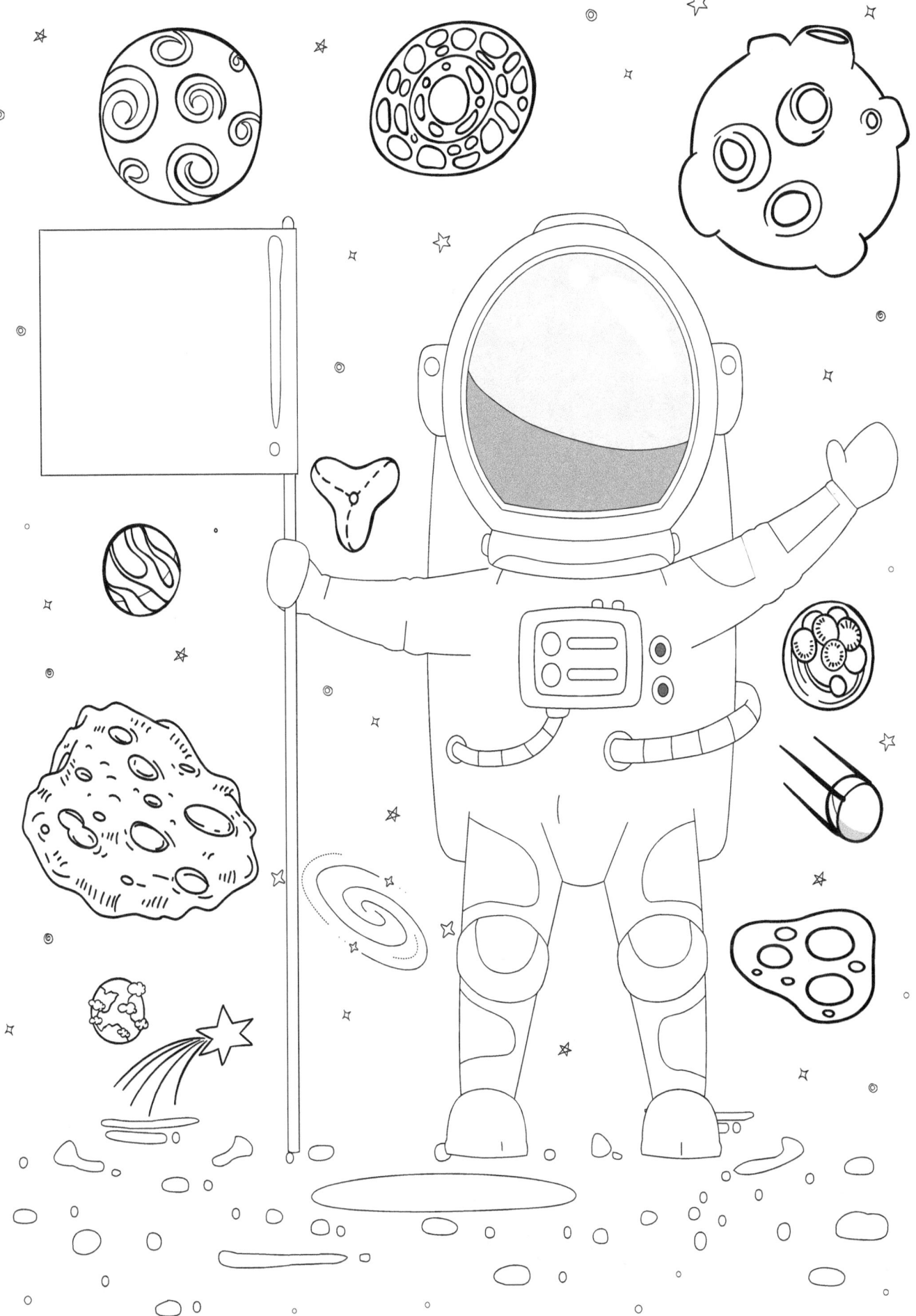

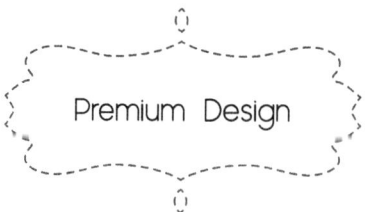

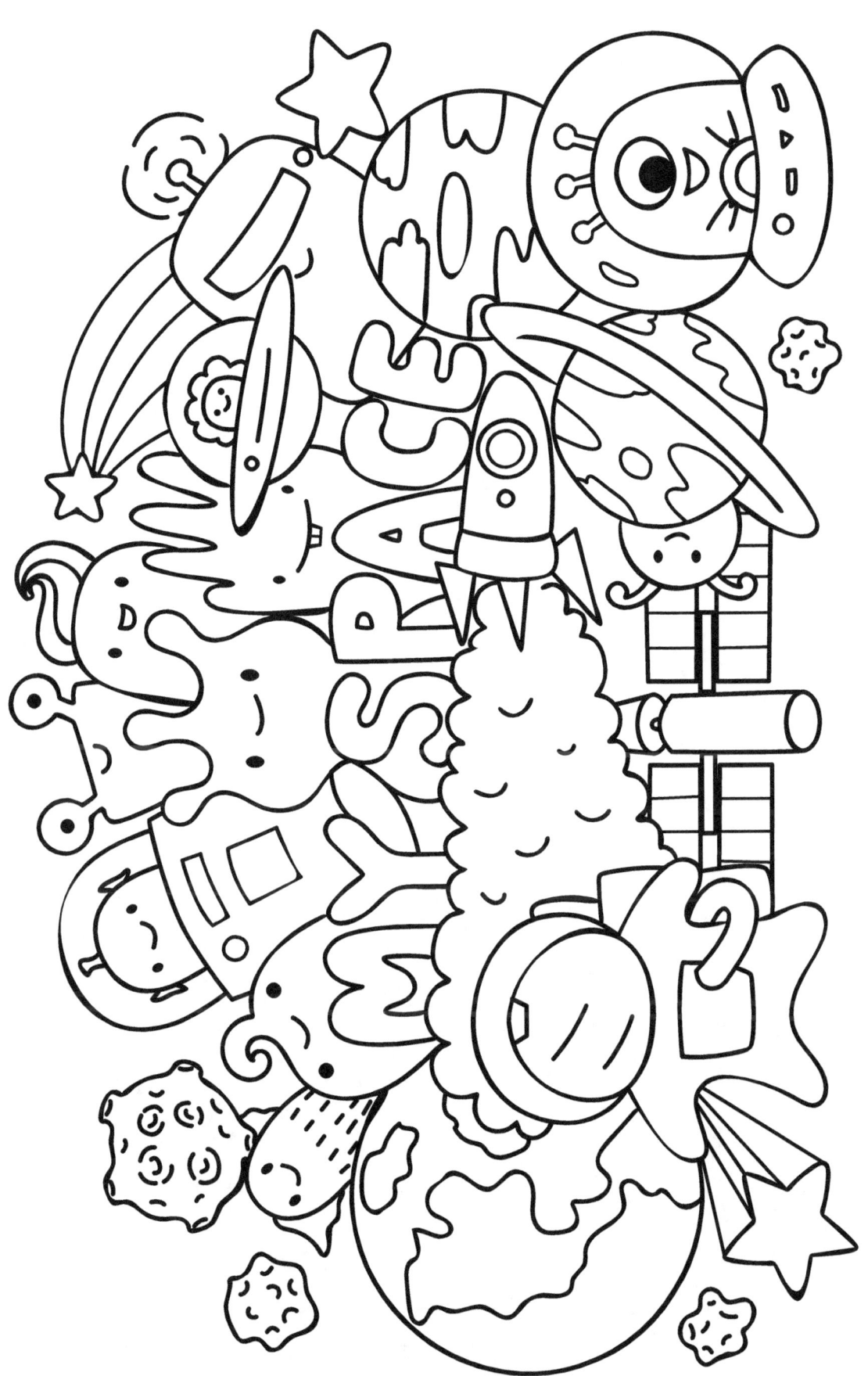

Premium Design

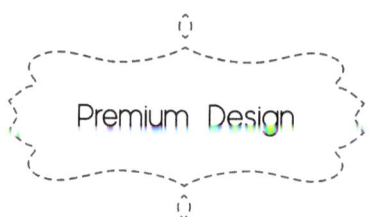